I0490934

Money Management Made Easy:

A Step-by-Step Guide to Financial Freedom

By

Peter B. Flores

Copyright @ by **Peter B. Flores** 2023. All rights reserved

Before this document is duplicated or reproduced in any manner, the publishers consent must be gained. Therefore, the content within can neither be stored electronically, transferred nor kept in a database.

Neither I part nor I full can the document be copied, scanned, fixed, or retained without approval from the publisher or creator.

TABLE OF CONTENTS

INTRODUCTION TO MONEY MANAGEMENT.................................1

CHAPTER ONE...3

    BUDGETING.. 3

CHAPTER TWO..5

    SAVING MONEY... 5

CHAPTER THREE...7

    SMART SPENDING..7

CHAPTER FOUR...9

    CREDIT MANAGEMENT...9

CHAPTER FIVE... 12

    INVESTING.. 12

    RETIREMENT PLANNING...15

    FINANCIAL LITERACY...18

CONCLUSION.. 21

INTRODUCTION TO MONEY MANAGEMENT

Money management is a crucial skill for anyone to develop in order to achieve financial success. It involves making decisions about how to use your money wisely and effectively, including budgeting, planning for future expenses, and investing. It also involves understanding how to make the most of your income, setting and meeting financial goals, and tracking your progress. Money management is an important part of financial health and well-being, and it is essential for achieving financial independence.

Money management involves understanding the different aspects of money and its role in our lives. This includes understanding the basics of saving and investing, as well as learning how to use money wisely and responsibly. It also involves understanding how to plan for the future and make smart financial decisions. Money management is not only important for achieving financial goals, but it also helps us to live within our means and develop strategies to cope with unexpected financial situations.

In addition to understanding the basics of money management, it is important to have an effective plan for managing your finances. This includes setting goals, creating budgets, tracking spending, and monitoring progress towards achieving financial goals. It also involves learning about different types of investments, such as stocks and bonds, and understanding the risks and rewards associated with each option.

Money management is a skill that requires knowledge, discipline, and commitment, and it is an important part of financial success. It is important to remember that money management is not a one-time event, but a continual process of learning, monitoring, and adjusting your financial plan as needed. By developing and following an effective money management plan, you can increase your financial security and set yourself up for a successful future.

CHAPTER ONE

BUDGETING

Budgeting is an important tool for money management that helps individuals, families, and businesses track incomes, expenses, and savings. It is a process of creating a plan for how money will be used and saved over a certain period of time. It helps people to better understand their financial situation and make more informed decisions about their finances.

Budgeting starts with assessing one's current financial situation, including income and expenses. Income includes any money that one receives, such as wages, salary, bonuses, investments, and other forms of income. Expenses can include housing costs, loan payments, groceries, entertainment, transportation, and any other expenses. After assessing all income and expenses, a budget should be created that takes into account all of these items and allows for some room for savings.

The budget should be realistic and flexible to account for unexpected expenses or changes in income over time. It should also be divided into different categories to make it easier for one to identify where their money is going and how it is being used. Categories may include housing, food, transportation, entertainment, savings, and other categories that are relevant to one's life.

Once a budget has been created, it can be used to monitor and adjust income and expenses to ensure that one is not spending more than they can afford. This can be done by tracking spending throughout the month and comparing it to the budget to ensure that one is staying within their budget. If spending exceeds the budget, adjustments should be made to ensure that one is not going over budget.

Budgeting is an important tool for money management and can help individuals, families, and businesses better understand their finances and make more informed decisions about their money. It can also help to ensure that one is not spending more than they can afford and can help them achieve their financial goals.

CHAPTER TWO

SAVING MONEY

Saving money is an important part of money management and financial security. The purpose of saving money is to have the resources needed to cover unexpected expenses, build a financial cushion, and achieve long-term financial goals. By setting aside a portion of your income each month, you can build a cushion to help protect you against financial hardship and set aside money for future goals.

The most important part of saving money is to start small and build up over time. Start by putting aside a small amount of money each month from your income. Try to boost your savings as your income rises. Automating your savings can help you stay on track, as the money is taken out of your account before you even have a chance to spend it.

Saving money is a great way to build a financial cushion for the future. Having an emergency fund is important for covering unexpected expenses, such as a medical bill or car repair. It can also help you cover costs if you lose your job or income unexpectedly. Having a financial cushion can give you peace of mind and provide financial security.

Saving money is also an important way to achieve your long-term financial goals. Whether it's buying a house, going on vacation, or saving for retirement, setting aside a portion of your income each month can help you reach your goals faster. If you invest your savings, you can take advantage of the power of compounding and have a larger sum of money when you need it.

Saving money is a great way to build financial security and reach your long-term goals. Start small and build up over time, and automate your savings to make sure you stay on track. With disciplined saving, you can have the resources you need when you need them.

CHAPTER THREE

SMART SPENDING

Smart spending is a type of money management that emphasizes making wise decisions with the money that you have available. It allows you to make informed decisions that will help you to stretch your budget and make your money go further. Smart spending involves setting a budget, tracking spending, and making conscious decisions about how you spend your money.

Setting a budget is an important part of smart spending. Making a budget helps you to get a clear picture of how much money you have to spend and how much you need to save. It also helps you to prioritize your spending so that you can make sure that your money is going towards the things that are most important to you.

Tracking spending is another key component of smart spending. Keeping track of your spending can help you to stay on budget and identify areas where you can adjust your spending to save money. Tracking expenses also allows you to see where your money is going and make informed decisions about where to allocate your money.

Making conscious decisions about how you spend your money is the core of smart spending. This involves taking the time to evaluate each purchase and determine if it is a good use of your money. It also involves considering the long-term impact of each purchase, such as whether it will save you money in the future or if it is something that you will use and enjoy for a long time.

Smart spending can help you to manage your money in a way that is both effective and sustainable. By setting a budget, tracking spending, and making conscious decisions about how you spend your money, you can make sure that your money is going towards the things that are most important to you and that you are making the most of your money.

CHAPTER FOUR

CREDIT MANAGEMENT

Credit management is the process of managing the use of credit cards and other types of credit accounts to ensure that the user is able to maintain their financial stability and make informed decisions when it comes to their finances. It involves understanding how to properly manage credit accounts, develop a budget, and make payments on time. It also involves understanding how to handle debt and how to use credit responsibly.

Credit management is important for money management because it helps individuals understand the importance of budgeting and debt management. When individuals understand how credit works and how to manage their credit accounts, they are better able to stay on top of their finances and avoid excessive debt. It also allows them to use their credit to their advantage, such as by obtaining lower interest rates, building credit, and taking advantage of promotional offers.

Good credit management also involves understanding the importance of having a good credit score. A good credit score is important because it affects an individual's ability to get loans and other forms of credit. A strong credit score can open up more opportunities to obtain credit, as well as help to lower interest rates.

Credit management also involves understanding the different types of credit available. This includes understanding the difference between secured and unsecured credit, as well as understanding the different interest rates and terms associated with each type of credit. Understanding these differences will help individuals make informed decisions when it comes to their finances and credit.

Finally, credit management also involves understanding the different types of credit card fees and charges. Credit card fees and charges can include annual fees, late fees, and over-limit fees. Understanding how to manage these fees can help individuals avoid overspending and ensure that they are not paying more than they should.

Overall, credit management is an important part of money management because it helps individuals understand how to manage their credit accounts, stay on top of their finances, and use their credit responsibly. It also helps individuals understand the importance of having a good credit score and how to manage their credit card fees and charges. By understanding these different aspects of credit management, individuals are better able to make informed decisions when it comes to their finances.

CHAPTER FIVE

INVESTING

Investing is a form of money management that involves placing funds into various financial assets with the primary goal of generating a return. Investing can be done in a variety of ways and is often used to build wealth over time. Investing can involve a variety of financial products including stocks, bonds, mutual funds, ETFs, commodities, and real estate.

When it comes to investing, the most important concept to understand is the concept of risk and reward. This means that the potential to make money through investing comes with the risk of losing money. When an investor chooses to invest their money, they should be aware of the risks associated with each investment and how those risks can affect their overall return. Additionally, it is important to have a clear understanding of the amount of money that can be lost in the event of a market downturn.

Before investing, investors should also consider their individual financial goals. For example, if an investor has a long-term goal of building wealth, they may choose to invest in assets that have the potential to generate higher returns over the long-term, such as stocks and mutual funds. Conversely, if an investor has a short-term goal of preserving their capital, they may choose to invest in assets that are more conservative, such as bonds or money market accounts.

When investing, it is also important to diversify. This means that an investor should spread their investments across multiple asset classes in order to reduce their overall risk. This can be done through investing in a range of different stocks, bonds, mutual funds, ETFs, commodities, and real estate. Additionally, investors should consider different types of investments such as stocks, bonds, real estate, and commodities, as each asset class carries its own set of risks and rewards.

Finally, it is important to practice proper money management when investing. This means that investors should be aware of the amount of money they are investing and the amount of money they are willing to risk. Additionally, investors should also be mindful of their budget and how much money they can afford to invest in order to ensure that they are investing responsibly.

Overall, investing is an important form of money management that can be used to build wealth over time. It is important to understand the risks associated with each investment and to have a clear understanding of one's individual financial goals before investing. Additionally, it is important to diversify one's investments and to practice proper money management when investing.

CHAPTER SIX

RETIREMENT PLANNING

Retirement planning is an important part of money management. It involves making decisions about how to save and invest for the future when you will no longer be working and earning an income. Retirement planning can help ensure that you have enough money to live comfortably when you retire, and it can also help you reach other financial goals.

The first step in retirement planning is to determine how much money you will need in retirement. This includes considering factors such as how much you will need to cover your basic living expenses, how much you will need for health care and other unforeseen costs, and how much you want to leave for your children or other heirs. Once you know how much money you will need in retirement, you can begin to create a plan for how to get there.

One key part of retirement planning is setting up a retirement savings account, such as an IRA or 401(k). This allows you to invest your money and take advantage of tax benefits, such as tax-deferred growth and the ability to contribute pre-tax dollars. You can also set up an automatic contribution plan so that money is automatically transferred from your paycheck into your retirement savings account. This helps to ensure that you are consistently saving for retirement.

Another important element of retirement planning is to diversify your investments. This means having a variety of investments such as stocks, bonds, mutual funds, and other types of investments. Diversifying your investments can help you to spread out your risk and reduce the impact of market downturns. It is also important to review your investments regularly to make sure that they are still in line with your goals.

Finally, retirement planning also involves planning for how you will withdraw money from your retirement savings. Generally, you can begin to withdraw money from your IRA or 401(k) after age 59 ½ without penalty.

You can also choose to rollover your account into a Roth IRA or other retirement account, which can provide additional tax benefits. It is important to consider the tax implications of your withdrawal plan before making any decisions.

Retirement planning is an important part of money management. It can help ensure that you have enough money to live comfortably in retirement and reach other financial goals. By creating a plan and setting up a retirement savings account, diversifying your investments, and planning for withdrawals, you can make the most of your money and secure your financial future.

CHAPTER SEVEN

FINANCIAL LITERACY

Financial literacy is the understanding of various financial concepts and the ability to make informed decisions around personal finances. It includes knowledge of financial concepts, such as budgeting, saving, investing, debt management, and retirement planning. Having financial literacy can help individuals to better manage their money and make informed decisions about their financial future.

The first step to good money management is understanding the basics of personal finance. This includes understanding basic financial concepts, such as budgeting, saving, and investing. Budgeting involves tracking income and expenses and creating a plan to manage money. Saving involves setting aside money for future needs, such as retirement or a major purchase. Investing involves putting money into financial products, such as stocks and bonds, in order to grow wealth over time.

Debt management is also an important part of financial literacy. This involves understanding how debt works, the different types of debt, and how to manage debt responsibly. It also involves understanding the risks associated with taking on debt and how to avoid it.

Retirement planning is an important part of financial literacy. This includes understanding how retirement savings work, the different types of retirement savings accounts, and how to create a retirement plan. It also involves understanding the tax implications of retirement savings and how to maximize returns.

Finally, financial literacy also involves understanding how to use financial products and services. This includes understanding the different types of financial products and services, such as loans, credit cards, and investments, and how to use them responsibly. It also involves understanding the risks associated with using these products and services and how to avoid them.

Overall, financial literacy is an important skill to have in order to effectively manage money and make informed decisions about personal finances.

Having financial literacy can help individuals to better manage their money and make informed decisions about their financial future.

CONCLUSION

Money management is a skill that is essential for everyone. It requires knowledge of budgeting, saving, investing, and creating financial security. Having a good understanding of money management can help reduce debt and stress, as well as helping to create a financially secure future. Money management is not just about spending, but also about planning, setting goals, and making wise decisions.

No matter what our financial situation is, it is important to learn and practice good money management habits. Having a budget, setting realistic financial goals, and understanding our financial options can help us make wiser financial decisions. It is also important to understand how to make the most of our money, by investing wisely and saving for the future.

Money management is a skill, and like any other skill, it must be learned and practiced. With the right knowledge and habits, we can use our money to create financial security and peace of mind.

It is essential to understand the basics of money management and to develop strategies that can help us make the most of our money. By doing so, we can ensure that we are living our best financial life.

www.ingramcontent.com/pod-product-compliance
Lightning Source LLC
Chambersburg PA
CBHW071149220526
45467CB00015B/2148